AT THE YE

AT THE YEAR'S ELBOW

Anne Higgins

Illustrations by
Maureen Beitman

Wipf & Stock
PUBLISHERS
Eugene, Oregon

Wipf and Stock Publishers
199 W 8th Ave, Suite 3
Eugene, OR 97401

At The Year's Elbow
Poems by Anne Higgins
By Higgins, Anne
Copyright©2000 by Higgins, Anne
ISBN: 1-59752-554-5
Publication date 2/1/2006
Previously published by The Edwin Mellen Press, 2000

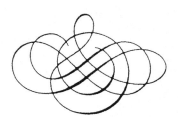

Contents

Part One: At the Year's Elbow

Part Two: Remarking the Texture

Part Three: The Shape of Night

Part Four: Birding

Part Five: Borders

Part Six: A Rose of Saints

Part One: At the Year's Elbow

At The Year's Elbow

September smells in the air
like school,
like the first awareness
of freedom's limits,
of the inevitable
snow.
Still green leaves
elegant with lacy
bug eaten holes,
rustle in the
still warm sun.
A bug runs up your arm
and changes directions
at September,
at your elbow,
the year's elbow.

A slight body language of wind,
a gesture of paling light says
Yes,
you are here
at the year's elbow.
In the morning,
the children
will go back to school.
In the evening,
the light will move away
with satchels
of flowers.

The Missing Children

Their faces stare up
at me
from the side
of cereal boxes,
from blue stamped
postcards.
Have you seen this child?
And now the age-enhanced
replica
of their faces
five years later,
with longer bones,
a futile hope,
for we know that they are
part of the forest ground,
where their hair and nails grow
long alone.
Or they have gone
through the Pied Piper's door
in some mountain,
living in bondage,
forgetting themselves.

Red Maple Keys

Backlighted,
they are fine grained silk.
Embryo of seed
like a quotation mark,
meets its twin
across the thin stem.
Inside is a tree
that will pump water from the earth,
defying gravity,
singing in the forest wind,
surrendering itself
into house, chair,
paper for a poem.

Deprived of Speech

The woman who smoked
her lungs away
and the woman who had a stroke
both lost the air
for the blood
that fed the mysterious room
in their heads
where speech was produced
like a factory,
a knitting factory,
a knitting machine,
swift and efficient,
effortless, seamless,
where all the wool
shorn from
the sheep of days,
the gathering of sleep,
was spun, colored, threaded,
woven, folded,
and delivered
as sweaters of laugher,
scarves of lies,
blankets of compassion,
coats of narration,
magnificent gloves
of memory,
delicate, precise
tatting of names.

Somewhere in there,
the starving machinery
shut down.

The wool piles up,
comes out of her mouth
in clumps of pronouns
that we must spin clumsily,
knit roughly,
holding the needles
awkwardly.

Cherry Tomatoes

Suddenly it is August again, so hot,
breathless heat.
I sit on the ground
in the garden of Carmel,
picking ripe cherry tomatoes
and eating them.
They are so ripe that the skin is split,
so warm and sweet
from the attentions of the sun,
the juice bursts in my mouth,
an ecstatic taste,
and I feel that I am in the mouth of summer,
sloshing in the saliva of August.
Hummingbirds halo me there,
in the great green silence,
and my own bursting heart
splits me with life.

Raisins

The vineyards tumble
down hills
like children
in the summer evening
before their parents
call them to bed.

The vineyards green and heavy
promise wine,
glinting secret is casks,
or raisins,
the disappointed ones,
the grapes
who settled for less.

Raise sins!
Rays ins,
wrinkled and sweet,
fly like,
sticking together
in boxes.
Dry and dark,
poor raisins,
never wine,
no longer young
and full of juice.
Over sweet
memory of summer
in mince pies.

The Ocean Speaks

A little girl is wading into me.
She looks into my blue beauty.
She does not look back.
She ruffles up my edges.
The white of my floor caresses her feet.
I swallow her shadow,
and soon
I will swallow her.
I will take her brightly colored circle away,
her life preserver that is only a toy.
I will stroke her blades and furrows,
her glossy hair will float in the blue of my depths,
silky and wet.
She will forget the shore.

Stopover

Brick mirage
in the flat stretch
of parking lots,
the Trailways bus station rises,
 a solid oasis
for those on the road.
For the natives,
it disappears
into the general route
to the library
or the grocery store.

The inside,
between buses,
is as dark as a desert outpost,
stung by the smell of french fries,
diesel oil,
soothed by the throbbing radio,
the regular breathing of the Coke machine,
the foreign language of
arrivals and departures.

The local madwoman
makes it real.
She speaks a familiar accent,
but she braces the walls
like a sentry.
She asks me for money as I walk by -
my payment
for staying home.

Anne Sexton's Last Reading

Seven years later I remember
the long red dress
clinging to your lanky frame,
a slash of blood
in the middle of the stage.
Your poems, too,
like slashes of blood.
How impolite of me
to stare at them.
You hung them in the air
with your
low nonchalant voice,
arranged them with
garish foreign hands,
garnished them
with cigarette smoke.
"Unless God keep the city,
the watchman watches in vain."
You said it was from Kennedy.
Now I know it is a psalm,
and now I know
that two days later,
you killed yourself
in a closed garage
with poison smoke
unnoticed by the watchman.
Rains of my regret
cannot wash
the blood from
your poems.

Four Thousand Suppers

At the kitchen table
at six o'clock.
Dark winter evenings
with my father in his winter underwear,
quilted like an astronaut.
Blue summer evenings
after my mother called my name
on the lilting breeze
which reached me
at far corners of the neighborhood,
her voice known
among all the others.

We ate
four thousand suppers
in that small room together.
What did we discuss?
Linoleum and carpet,
casement windows,
the wild McElroys,
the loud Mrs. Supportas,
scenes from the fifth grade,
my problems with bushels and pecks.

Four thousand suppers -
oceans of tea.
The man and woman at the table
grow grey.
I grow up -
feet finally
reach the floor.

In the English Class

We are reading
Julius Caesar,
and as we read,
the boy in the third row
grows before my eyes
like time lapse photography.
There's a clock within him
that went off today
with an alarm so high
he cannot hear it.

Even as we read,
the bones are growing
around the book
in his lengthening fingers.
His skin is pink and rough
with stretching bones.
The alarm wakes his face,
changing the cheekbones,
making them long and flat,
his father's face.
The nose lengthens
from child's anonymity
into the family nose,
his father's face
which I have seen
in the afternoons
behind the windows
of the car.

Irrevocable

I sing of the lost things
that cannot be found,
the tiny key to the file,
the slides of the building that's five years
torn down,
the photo of the woman
ten years dead.

I sing of the broken things
that cannot be mended:
the tulip blossom torn to the ground
by the heartless child,
the egg seeping
out of the carton,
the film exposed to the light,
the coat lining ripped
at the center,
not the seam.

Part Two: Remarking the Texture

:; there is no escape.
rned ruins of the night;
:ch by color but by shape.

' in number, shrink in size.
ll us closer to the light.
:. There is no escape.

The broken sky compels us to awake;
the scattered shreds of mountains dim our sight;
They do not match by color but by shape.

Remark the texture of the curves and planes.
Stand back and focus mystery's delight;
Begin the puzzle; there is no escape.

The New Year dawns upon the ritual;
We put the sky together, fitted tight;
It does not match by color, but by shape.

We feel and test; we fail and find. We rise.
Return the picture to component shards:
Begin the puzzle. There is no escape.
It does not match by color, but by shape.

Head First

Eight years old,
sleek as a seal in my
shiny wet swimsuit,
I climb the ladder
to the high diving board.

Eight feet up,
balanced by thick summer air,
I slowly bend and see,
depths down,
the glacier pool.

Eight o'clock
on the summer evening,
the sun throws
sheets of satin
over the water.
A distant radio runs mandolin music...
Our day will come...
You're sure to fall in love...

I think of pirates,
of tumbles down stairs,
of flying.
A quick breath
like a leaf,
and splash

Wisteria and Foxglove

Wisteria
hanging down from the twirling vines,
your perfume sways
from purple clusters
into the spicy air.

Foxglove
pink bells reaching up to a tilting tower
along the garden walk,
stalactites fragile as water,
I walk among you.

What hangs down
out of my vines,
blooming purple,
perfuming the air?
What words of mine
reach up,
blooming like bells,
defined and precise as stalactites,
framing the path?

I leave the gravel path
and walk
where the foxgloves brush my legs.
My hands cup themselves
around the bowls
of wisteria.

Palm Reading

One June I rode
a helicopter
over country roads
in Pennsylvania.

This landscape
wears round hills
and three intersecting roads
with thin tree lined lanes,
hair thin,
lightly etched from their stem.
A deep comforting river
curves left
down to
wrist and vein.

Hidden right
in the unpaved
hill country,
buried lead
from the stabbing
of a child.

It is drought time,
callous time.
The main intersection
joins life and hope:
one traced,
one carved.

View From Behind

Tapestries look
like battlefields
from the back.
Threads like soldiers
in hand to hand combat -
who is most resilient?
Arms locked, elbows out,
clenched fists of knot
scattered
like small skirmishes
across the expanse.
Who is most flexible?
Stitches quarrel
in overbearing voice,
rush to trenches,
maintain positions.
Colors invade
each others' territory,
singing violent
victories
of light.
All clamor, all struggle,
it faces the wall of faith
while the weaver
and the watcher
work from the front.

The Lighthouse at Point Reyes

The road winds out to the end of the west,
where the west falls into fog,
into rock and slate water,
startled seals raise their heads out of the slatey sea.

The road winds out to the end of the west,
curving and covering and turning its shoulder
where the sun shines on blue water,
shrugging at the ghosts of fog and mist.

Ghostly mists roll the brushy hills,
the undulating road, ruffle wildflowers and cliffs
out of the fog and into the blue west
where the sun shines over the next hill,
where the dead wait over the next hill,
opening their hands to the lotion of the fog,
opening their ears to the song of the seals
on the west's last wind.

Drafting Shadows

When the architect
planned the church,
did he ever stand on
the bare ground
at nine on a sunny morning
in February,
and see where his shadow fell?
Did he envision that sun
tilting through windows,
high windows,
hitting the huge cross
so that its shadow
struck the far wall
just as people were saying
"He has come to his people
and set us free."

Could he in his mind
measure how high
to place those windows
with some geometry
of the imagination,
up in the invisible wall
below the invisible dome,
placing an hypotenuse
of sunbeam
into the mosaic of
an enormous eye?

Recipe

Yeast rises
like praise
clings to the cloth,
leaves its thready face there.

Dough rolls smooth
springs back
seamless in hand
as thought.

The oven opens and closes
its arms.
Smell seeps
from room to room.

Bread, as finished
as a child.
Every slice of the knife
it sings its fearful litany:
I live in the jaws of hunger.
I break as I give
I rise as I die.

Open-Hearted

A nest of tubes,
a cradle of monitors,
someone in there
whose breastbone has been pulled open
like French Doors,
and whose heart, almost broken,
has been handled,
and laid bare,
in front of strangers.

Heart laid bare,
the weakest walls exposed
and shored up,
clogged arteries
discovered and cleared.
Heart handled,
put back
for its red roots
to settle.

The days after,
each beat wonders
will I live?
Every breath hurts.
The months after, each beat waits
for the seals to set,
for the scar,
like a mummy's mouth,

silent ceiling over the
hidden stitches,
to pale a little,
to flatten and soften its grimace
a little.
The years after,
street clothes hide it,
hide the question
will I walk?
Will this heart sustain me
in the sprints of joy,
the sweats of panic?

The psalm says
Open hearted,
the good person gives to the poor.
We stand,
survivors of less visible repairs,
looking in at the nest of tubes,
following the arpeggio of beats
on the monitor.

Strong Coffee

Strong coffee
smells like a current
of warm southerly air
in the climate of dawn.
Strong coffee
gets stronger
when poured back
through the grounds.
Opaque,
thick, hot, bitter
for waking up,
the caffeine
pumps through your center,
stains your mouth with morning,
with going to work,
surprises you
with your own
breath.

The Crooked Path

Sinuous and brown as a snake,
weaving through the furry grass
leading from the wilderness
to the industrial park,
to the fruit packaging plant.
How is a place that packages nature
called a plant?
Plant means daffodils,
dieffenbachias...
But plant also means
a building made of concrete block...
Plant also means
a person placed deliberately somewhere
to spy,
or to ask a contrived question...
Plant also means
to place something somewhere -
an idea, a bulb,
something green and potted,
something flesh and blood,
something listening.

In Tandem

The fact is: when you ride in front, you steer.
The person in the back controls the speed.
The pedals go as quickly as they need
to keep one's partner accurate with fear.
A panic on the handlebars will clear
confusion as to who will take the lead.
The person who relinquishes is freed
to stabilize the pair, and mere
agreement brings a rush of calm and peace
as widely round the corners they can glide,
adjusting speed and vision with each turn.
Exhilaration, energy, release
accompany their willingness to ride;
reward them with the pace for which they yearn.

Part Three: The Shape of Night

The Shape of Night

In the middle of the night
when the air is filled with water
and I swim in a dark pool of sleep,
in the deepest part of that forest
there is something
that doesn't have a name.
I wake because I heard
someone calling that name
inside me.
In this forest
which grew where I did not plant it,
or plan it,
I swim in a green cellar,
breathing water,
diving deeply
into my name.

In this dream
I sew my poem to God
inside my clothes,
my night clothes,
like Blaise Pascal.
The paper rubs
against my chest
like a dry mustard plaster,
getting soft
as cloth again.

Played from Memory

Night opens his mouth -
baritones a breath of stars.
The square sky
over the courtyard
dusted with sound.

In tonight's program,
a quick polonaise
between symphonies.
A shooting star
flashes a bright note
struck once,
alone.
Like a zipper of light,
it slides down the scale
into silence.

Compunction

The leaves lie thick
as guilt
in the back yard,
hard acorns
of regret
sinking into
the earth,
hard to walk on
as hot coals.

Crossing the Alps

We are standing still.
The trees race
by the black backs
of mountains
rolling on the full mooned sky.
They are candle shadows
on cathedral walls.

The wind,
pouring air on the train,
tastes sweet
and cold as water.

Standing world
in a darkroom,
night reversed by the moon -
by the moon!
What lies behind that sky
not dark wood of worlds
but light.
We know
by the singular hole
of a star.

DaVinci and Manet

What lines in the eye
convey the calm fortress?
Resistance to entry?
Leonardo cannot conquer
the guarded heart of Ginevra de Benci,
so he paints one flake of light
into her flawless pebble
of pupil,
revealing the wall
of her sturdy and exquisite
self absorption.

What lakes of light in the eye
convey the reservoir of tears?
Set in the fair skin
below furry fronds of red hair,
the eyes of the nameless barmaid
at the Folies Bergers
invite Manet
to swim in those lakes of
unmistakeable sadness,
and Manet takes us with him
into them
forever.

A Hunting Scene

Hunter
long shadow on the left
leaving houses behind the horizon.
White shoulders of roof, brown belly of earth,
pulling the gun into the trashed land,
palpable presence in the brush,
Prey.

Kafka

for Ralph Harper

The man from the country
sits at the door of the law.

The corridor is quiet.
The door is closed.
He has written
a wordless poem
in his head
while he waits.

He wonders
about a translator,
about a publisher.
The poem wonders
about chalkboard,
snow,
dust in the corner.

A sound comes at last -
a squeak somewhere.
A light wind on his face
indicates that somewhere
a door has opened,
old on its hinges.
He will get lost
finding it.

In the Walters Art Gallery:
The Temptation in Eden

It meets you on the central stairs -
Della Robbia's life sized wreath
in glazed white porcelain.
Olive green leaves
decked with yellow pears,
frame Adam and Eve
deciding.
The serpent,
large as a python,
capable of swallowing them both,
winds herself round
the Tree
of the Knowledge of Good and Evil.
The serpent's porcelain arms
twist invitingly,
hands offer the shining fruit.

From one angle,
Eve looks interested;
Adam, somnolent,
the serpent, earnest.

Della Robbia gave
Eve and the serpent
identical blonde faces.

Thief

He kicked the door open.
Deadbolt splintered
the wooden frame.

He took everything
he could carry -
everything
he could sell.

I came home
to a door hanging open,
a note from the police.

The next night
I lay in bed listening
to cars cough to a start,
tires hiss through the green light,
solitary drunk voice
cry like a night bird.
I lay there
in my shoes,
dressed to run.

Jack London's House Warming

Wolf House lurks alone
like a Mayan temple
in the forest of the Valley of the Moon,
waiting for Jack London
to host his first party there.
At midnight,
the owl rides the rafters, searching stone
for shadowy mice
who run the rough boulders.
Deer pick their way to the tender grass
that grows in the empty swimming pool.
Wolves reclaim the ballroom.

Remains from the inferno,
brown boulders, volcanic rock,
rough hewn and heavy,
miss the tree torsos
that walled them
that joined them.
All the tiles gone , all the redwoods gone,
burned in the fire of the
wedding night of the house,
fire reaching its arms out,
flames embracing,
smoke whispering its name
in the calm August midnight,
flames that waited all their lives
for such a feast.

Part Four: Birding

The Least Terns

In June they build
their skimpy nests
on the sand.
Overhead, they hover,
white commas on the blue page of sky,
pause in their diving
to threaten us
with their dreadful talons.
We shrink, instead,
from their extinction.

At Cape May

At the bird sanctuary
in mid-September,
a million silver
tree swallows
wallow and swoop in the air,
taking great swallows of air,
folding up on the tall stalks
of marsh weeds
like shining Christmas ornaments.
As one,
they flash like a flag
of silver and slate blue
against the turbulent
cerulean sky,
unfurling south.

Chickadee

Chickadee,
quick as a retort,
snatches one
sunflower seed,
tilts his sleek
black mask
to watch me,
then sharply
angles
into the air,
buzzing a rebuke.

Killdeer

Thin, gentle,
longlegged killdeer
built her nest
in rocks on the parking lot.
Four or five large
black-brown speckled eggs
waited
under a portable sign.

As I approached,
the mother called,
flew low,
landed before me,
dragging her wings
and playing hurt
to lure me away from her nest.

How many predators
would fall
for such an act?
And who can fold
the wings of defense
in the face of
uninvited visitors?

Rubythroat

Iridescent green
Pegasus for Thumbelina,
rapier between enormous onyx eyes,
your wing sounds only in silence.
I feel the agitation of air,
your sudden presence in my face.

I search in vain
for your thimble sized nest,
Spun by you of spidersilk,
firmly fixed on a finger of dogwood.

In April,
I wait for your return from the tropics.
I hope you survived
the hurricane winds
and the spring storms
light as you are,
as you crossed
and recrossed
the Gulf of Mexico.

Merlin

The memory moves faster than the pen.
The merlin lands minutely on the wire,
But flashes off in sunlight as I near.

Behind my eyes are attics full of rooms
whose only access lies in photographs
The merlin lands minutely on the wire.

That window overlooking maple trees,
where winter sunsets blazed in molten red,
It flashes off in sunlight as I near.

The snowbird that I rescued Easter day
lay stunned but blinking, heating up my hand.
The memory moves faster than the pen.

The morning kitchen silence breaks and hums,
The Rubythroat appears, and chirps and drinks,
he flashes off in sunlight as I near.

The face of one long dead begins to form.
I see his thick brown hair wave in the wind,
He flashes off in sunlight as I near.

The breath of God upon my neck, so clear
and sudden once in one of those close rooms..
The memory moves faster than the pen.

I reach into the ocean's briny mouth.
My hand emerges empty, wet with tears...
The memory moves faster than the pen.

Hawk Mountain

The sharp rock cut feet
when we swung out over the leather leaves.
The eye of the kestrel sharp
in the hot southeast wind.
Her throat closed on silence
kissed with her traveling.

Vultures curved lazily wavering
in the blue thermal swinging
below us,
tilted like black kites
between slag and red trees
kissed with unexpected heat.

Curved clouds hung over
the five peaks,
bruised the blue distances.
Our arms raised, pointing,
gasping as the determined
travelers swirled
silent worlds over our heads,
autumn eyes on the southern sky.

The Birdwatcher

Consumed in the sunshine
of a field full of loss,
Riding the gusts of memory,
I call to my sorrows,
elusive warblers,
who reply
from the tall grass,
occasional flash of gold,
cedar waxwings
calling from deep
in the green glen.
They're the ones I want to see.
I scorn the obvious
pigeons and starlings
who scavenge
at my feet.

Antiphon in the Style of Hildegard

O You Who
made the sharp shinned hawk
with red eyes
rend the singing sparrows
in the silent slice of death,
Who fill the sunset sky with
roses and crows,
Who paint the breast of the warbler
with flashes of Your Spirit,
and crown the finger small kinglet
with Your blood,
bless me with wonder
at the paradox of Your plans.
Like birds,
may my heart's croaks
and arias
praise You.

Part Five: Borders

Borders

"The Illusion of Borders:
the illusion that they are real,
and the grand illusion that they are not."
                    - Stanley Cavell

What separates the past from the present?
Touch the switch -
the man flies back
onto the diving board,
the border of air and water,
where dry becomes wet,
weight becomes feather,
sharp becomes silk.

Off the trunk, overhead the shirt,
back , back through the door,
heels first.

In the camera, we are
lintbeams in the light,
halted at the screen,
flattened on celluloid,
seeping out around the edges of the power button,
in some dark projection room.

"Where is our territory?"
We climb to the top of the frame,
slip back to the bottom,
hearing the twin dim heartbeat
from far above.

February Dawn

Orange wakes.
I stir and stretch my orange arms.
My toes touch
the edge of the sun.
Copper faucet pours orange,
Orange streams
through sun-bright glass,
Heats the cool green walls.
Bedspread patterns tropic,
swirling in the blaze.

The globe in the sky
turns white once more.
I button tired schoolclothes,
Sway out and away
on the icebound path -
but orange footprints burn
behind.

Orpheus and Euridice

Walking breathlessly
up the steep grade,
I press my arms close.
They would wave goodbye,
silence air, fragment light,
briefly banish the flies.

Behind, hear
the snakes hiss in her hair,
"You coward!"
Who could deny that wish to see?

Behind, smell
charred sharp Gomorrah burning
all my furniture.
I want to see the red glow of its going.

Behind, feel
the girl I sang back from the dead.
What color are her eyes?
What did they see in that long winter?
Her small hand in mine
grows warm.

Can I climb all the way without turning round once?
Can I believe in light, in desert,
in return?
This neck, held rigidly, hopefully forward,
is never so stiff
as stone.

Blizzard

The deaf snow speaks
in sign
like a prophet.
His fingers remark the landscape
swiftly, stolidly.
They say
This time I am serious.
He cups his thick hand
on the birdsnest,
levels the driveways,
leans on the trees,
pulls the sky down
to the earth - nebulae swirl
by the second story windows.
This time I am serious.
This time
you will hear me.

Advent

My sister crochets
an afghan for Christmas.
She ripped it out several times
before the center satisfied,
before the colors pleased.

She crochets quickly, deftly,
turning the work
at each new row.
The afghan covers her
from waist to foot
as she works.
The cancer inside
quickly, deftly
knots itself around her bones.

She crochets nimbly, quickly
with her bony hands
light as a fine
grey sparrow,
making a nest
bigger than herself.

The Dependency

Clinging to the back of the house in Charleston,
a crumbling ghost,
slave quarters empty a century.

Once, like a busy,
angry woman
grown out of her corset,
she bristled,
comparing the heat here
with Africa,
listening to the sun send
blasts of light
loud as tribal drums.

Now, she clings
reproachfully
to the big house.
Her brittle bones tremble
from the air conditioner,
itch with palmetto bugs
festering in the plaster.
Long iron rods
protect her spine
from earthquakes.
The alley shields her
from hurricanes.
She signals her presence
with hot
musty breath.

April Birth

I was born on a green day
with shoots of April green sparks
flashing in the trees.
Light green leaves pushing
white blossoms into flight.
Having just arrived,
olive green birds with white breasts
jumped from branch to branch.
The sun poured lime green smells
on the hands of the warm wind.
Grass green bugs began their march to summer.
I opened my tiny voice
and my newborn cry
was a green poem
to Tuesday afternoons.

The Space Window at the Washington Cathedral

In the midst of Gothic
pointing, stretching,
stone and smell of spring
window stories
of God
coming to earth,
is a breath-catching
view of earth
coming to God.
Here is glimpse, outside
our field
into deep of swirling
pinwheel planets and stars
in a Van Gogh, Hopkins
himmel hoch
and hosanna in excelsis
shining on us
in a bath of purple
Revelation,
unframed,
unstoned.

Penelope

Even after the chameleon turned
the color of night,
and the rain stopped,
I still sat at home with a light in the window -
I still sat at home with my hand on the pen.

Even after my speech became short
and the suitors grew loud in the street below,
I still sat on the great bed
watching the tree branches
disappear into the smoky ceiling.

And still I was waking from the same dream,
the one of rolling backwards in a carriage
down a mountain,
of wandering through halls,
doors into parallel halls,
strange slanted walls
where crying voices called
"He is gone,
he is gone."

Even after I knew
that the suitors lurked below
to lure my loneliness,
Still I planted flowers
in the backyard
where their horses' hooves
killed everything.

The Roofless Church

A poem on silence
sits on silence
like a leaf
on a still pool,
light, brittle,
brown as earth.

Silence,
brown as earth,
silence
we describe
by making
walls around it
and describing
the walls.

In the center
of that
roofless church,
a pear
whose seed
is God.

Watching the Plants Come Up

In early March,
the slow concentrated watching.
In the earliest
morning light,
hesitating to start
the trip to work,
I walk the rock garden,
staring at the short stalks
of daffodils
two inches out of the ground,
a tentative green,
a diffident green,
pushing out from under
the last crumbled
autumn leaves.
Embryonic leaves
of chrysanthemums,
green rosettes
of sedum
cluster around
last summer's
brown stalks.

More quickly than the crocus,
the bean seeds rise.
In the summer,
I watch them come up -

just their first strong
tiny green arms,
elbowing their way
out of the earth,
clot of earth still clinging.
The next morning,
a little leaf.

It is hard to open the car door,
and climb into its cold
gassy arms,
and go off to work
when each morning
a revelation waits
at home.

Smoke and Fire

"We've all of us got smoke and fire
and flames behind us."
                              - RIDDLEY WALKER

Places we ran from,
places we never want to
see again.
The heat burned the
inside of our noses
as we escaped
with only our lives.

Devastated areas
where we wonder
whether anything will
grow again.

In Yellowstone Park
one year after the
great conflagration,
deep blue and yellow
wildflowers grow
through the charcoal.
In the heart of the
fired wood,
something new blooms.

Part Six: A Rose of Saints

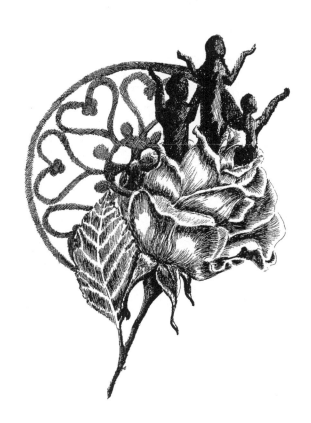

Canterbury Chartres

Sing blue light death,
burn maps of heaven
how can you so massive
be so light?
Feet fall in frozen
faces stone smooth
from the steps of people
smoothing centuries.

Shouting joy from the last pane
a blue plane of stained glass why
never finished,
soaring to the sky
Even the stone bones
push the lungs high
where the dragon winged
stretch a silent cry.
A march of martyrs,
a rose of saints
sing to the long still workman's hands:
Je l'aime qui donne avec joie.

The Villa Mass

The old sisters
sing at the Offertory:
Heart of Jesus, meek and mild,
in two part harmony,
words the world stopped singing
before we were born.
Blue veins, twig fingers,
voices like new bells
call Jesus.

His children,
their voices in the air
project old films:
limber legs rushing to school,
wool, starch,
waxing the floors by hand,
rising at four,
white linen,
long sicknesses
like grim guests
waiting in the parlor.

Their armies have gone
to a handful.
Now, we kneel behind them,
help them
to the altar
where we are
their only rail.

Visiting the Prison on Christmas Eve

The woman on the other side of the glass
is singing silent night along with me.
She sticks her brown hand through the food slot
and I hold her hand as we sing.
I look through the thick, smeared
bullet proof glass
into her brown almond eyes,
into sunsets over Aztec jungles,
and we are singing silent night.
Her eyes tell me she has babies at home
and she is crying and I am crying
and we sing silent night.

Rain on the Hedgerows

I do desire you, God.
Your touch like rain on my face,
rain on the landscape of my heart,
like a meadow full of weedy
brown late summer grass,
full of field sparrows,
tangled vines full of thorns and berries,
pokeberry, chokecherry, hackberry trees,
full of cedar waxwings,
your rain lingering like dew on that thicket
that is my heart,
that thicket of desires, thorns, thorny questions
and leaf-berry thick hidden places
where the warblers go to eat the purple berries
of my passions, my regrets, my dreams,
fears, imaginings,
a thick, overgrown path, Lord, wet with your rain,
growing and ripening all that fruit for your
Spirit to eat,
your Spirit in the wings
of a million birds passing through me.

Mary of Egypt
The Harlot of the Desert

Mary of Egypt
consumed by God
black, burned black as a cinder
by the sun of her longing,
thirst burned out of her throat,
hunger shrunk out of her belly.

Mary of Egypt, in an ecstasy of prayer,
floating above the desert floor, then,
running naked
across the hills of desert sand, then
dead, the charred life shed.

A lion stood by her body,
the lion of lust in the desert,
the lion amazingly tamed, standing wake at her
black cinder shed, lying dead
on the desert sand,
the lion tan and rough
as the sand,
his golden mane tamed,
dug her a grave
with his great tan paws.

The Daughter of Jairus

Only You can tell them
that I am only sleeping,
not dead,
all those women
who mourn for me
outside the door-
those ghosts,
those grandmothers,
guardians and celebrities -
tell them.
Only You
can sell me and keep me,
can call me
from the night behind my eyes.
I lie in an empty room
where the sun sends
her pillars gushing to the floor.
Only You
can wake me in
daylight's delight.
I have slept so late,
in the center of my body
is a glass full of rest.

Elizabeth Seton

Proud straight woman
with the snapping eyes,
you had to look up
to your benefactors.
You had to sail oceans
to make up your mind,
and lose all your lace
to be stubborn.
You had to be cold
in a damp stone house,
rubbing your hands together
before you could play
that piano,
and you had to wear black
enough
to understand.
Proud loving woman,
pulled into heaven
between last minute
reminders
to earth!

The Name of Now

for the Washington Theological Union

I used to be Jacob,
sleeping on my stone pillow,
but now I am Nicodemus,
asking you my questions by night.
I used to be Goliath,
felled by a stone to my arrogance,
but now I am Zaccheus,
scrambling down to meet you,
struck by the stone of your voice
calling my name.
I used to be Rebecca,
maneuvering you with my fake skin,
but now I am Magdalene,
racing with joy from the rolled away stone,
your voice rolling in my ears.

Your name retrieves all mysteries.
Your throat kisses the sharpest word.
I hear your name, and mine,
in syllables of color and shadow
carved together
out of air and electricity,
on the pillow of darkness.

I wake
in the light-filled room,
where wisdom places me
with living stones.
Now we form
a school for ministry.
We used to be in Athens,
but now we're in Jerusalem.

In the Phillips Gallery: The Repentent Peter

Goya and El Greco
both painted him.
Goya's man looks to the West -
up and forward, his melon face
bald, practical,
used to laughter.
Strong thick peasant arms
extend out
clasped to heaven,
keys set aside
on the arm of the sofa.

El Greco saw him
stretched,
with a long sad
poet's face,
shadowed cheeks,
eyes drawn down
at the outside corners,
looking East.
His clasped hands pull in
towards his heart;
the keys still
hooked to his belt.

These two
have just heard the cock crow.
They face each other
from the walls
of neighboring rooms in the gallery,
through a wide doorway.

Margaret

Her black Irish eyes,
practical as tile,
suddenly open like onyx wells
as she snaps out of sleep.
The ragged breath slips and then catches
on the edge of the cliff
from which she hangs,
and she's back in the bed, saying
What day is it?
What day?

It's the cusp of October,
humid, tropical,
storming through the long afternoon.
Delirious, she's letting old secrets
slip out around the oxygen mask.
She's emptying the last closets
where worries of the details
of graduations,
anguish of lost colleges,
irreplaceable keys,
quiver in the corners.

If the moon answers to the name
Old Woman Who Never Dies,
What should I call her,
whose waning hand holds mine
as she pulls away from me
into the air of the clean cold
Sunday morning?

Teresa at Lake Artemesia

When you get caught by the rain,
When you get caught in the rain,
When you realize
there's no hope
of reaching the car,
You just surrender
as the rain drenches you.
You surrender
as it soaks you to your core.
You relish the feeling
of the deep surprise,
of the dim sense of
seeds breaking open
somewhere in the dark.
You feel like dancing in the rain
with the thirsty earth.

Eventually you have to reach the car
and dry off,
but oh,
the wet laughter
of the meantime!

Acknowledgements

"At the Year's Elbow" SISTERS TODAY Sept.1982
"The Missing Children" ENGLISH JOURNAL April 1985
"Deprived of Speech" WEST WIND REVIEW May1996
"Raisins" ICARUS Spring 1977
"Stopover" CROSSCURRENTS June 1983
"Anne Sexton's Last Reading" FOUR QUARTERS
        Spring 1983
"In the English Class" COLLEGE ENGLISH Sept.1993
"Irrevocable" WEST WIND REVIEW May1996
"Jigsaw" YANKEE February 1983
"View from Behind" REVIEW FOR RELIGIOUS Jan.1982
"Drafting Shadows" REVIEW FOR RELIGIOUS March1995
"OpenHearted" FOUR QUARTERS Spring 1990
"Recipe" COMMONWEAL August 4, 1978
"February Dawn" LIT Winter, 1969
"Blizzard" SISTERS TODAY January 1980
"Advent" REVIEW FOR RELIGIOUS December 1993
"April Birth" REVIEW FOR RELIGIOUS April 1998
"The Space Window at the Washington Cathedral"
COMMONWEAL April 12, 1980
"Penelope" THE WIDENER REVIEW October 1997
"The Roofless Church" ANTIGONISH REVIEW
        Summer 1982
"Smoke and Fire" SISTERS TODAY March 1997
"Canterbury Chartres" SISTERS TODAY May1979
"The Villa Mass" REVIEW FOR RELIGIOUS Aug.1986
"Rain on the Hedgerows" SSJ LaGrange Calendar 1999
"The Daughter of Jairus" REVIEW FOR RELIGIOUS
        March 1981
"Elizabeth Seton" COMMONWEAL February 1976
"The Name of Now" WTU Program October 1997
"Margaret" COMMONWEAL Oct.23, 1998

"Rain on the Hedgerows" in A TIME TO GATHER—1999 calendar published by Sisters of St. Joseph of La Grange, Illinois.

"The Repentant Peter" in FROM EASTER TO PENTECOST by Robert Morneau, Spring 2000.

"Four Thousand Suppers" in FROM EASTER TO PENTECOST by Robert Morneau, Spring 2000.

About the Author

Anne Higgins was born in West Chester, Pennsylvania. She is a member of the Daughters of Charity. She is a graduate of Saint Joseph College, Emmitsburg, Maryland, The Johns Hopkins University, and the Washington Theological Union. She lives in Emmitsburg and teaches and works in campus ministry at Mount Saint Mary's College.

About the Illustrator

Maureen Beitman was born in Baltimore, Maryland. She is a member of the Daughters of Charity. She has studied at the Maryland Institute College of Art. She lives in Baltimore and works at Frederick Ozanam House, outreach for persons who are homeless.

Made in the USA
Las Vegas, NV
09 December 2022

61585226R00056